Hough & Helix & Where & Here
& You, You, You

Hough & Helix & Where & Here & You, You, You

by

Lea Graham

No Tell Books
Reston, VA

Published by No Tell Books, LLC
notellbooks.org

ISBN: 978-0-9826000-2-3

Editorial Consultant: Jill Alexander Essbaum

Cover Designer: Mary Behm-Steinberg

Proofreader: Roxanne Halpine Ward

Contents

For Kyle & Jay, crock pot beans & Stevie Wonder

Crushed: A Preface

The entire history of human desire takes about seventy minutes to tell.
Unfortunately, we don't have that kind of time.
—Richard Siken

Crushed by smack or cosh, by rubbernecking

              up against flapping, the brilliance of chickens

"to alter"

                              (4H, those county fairs)

  for Ronny Camareri & sturgeon moons

                        the postman rings twice

crushed

                 around neon

porque tú eres una pedazita de fruta

              once in a payphone, once in rain

a place where the dancing's free

                    beyond Exit 10, *The Amboys*

, nevertheless, Pete Gray

           by scale & proportion

              crushed when there's nothing else to say

"to burden (grievously)"

hence, Chicago's paper birch & brick

that night, the Cass Hotel

      in the slatch

if Aqua Velva, if Blue Waltz

     mornings, Mad Dog's electric blue

triangulates

    since "crush room" is about waiting

(I'm not a player I just crush a lot)

    behind your velvet Elvis

     & "stirs beyond your wall"

launches & ripples

    "in the absences of eyes"

     this canvas, that stone

Where to go from here?

     "within the precincts of the poem"

shouldn't be ugly

    yet, femurs, molars, cigarette cases

      their notebooks & teacups

(crushed)

"to crash, crowd, embrace"

as much, Lethe

    "to grind (as into particles)"

these narratives should know better:

       the Door of Paradise,

let the English in

    ice & silver spoons

"to subdue (completely); to suppress"

      (this will all be over soon)

inside letters, out in the shed

        careful, careful

    bloody palm to white sheet –

"to overwhelm (as if by weight; or confusion, humiliation)"

       before waffles

   Crushed imperative: *Turn the record over, pull off your wingtips!*

"to rumple, wrinkle, crease"

    "no sight & drumming"

       blind, relucent

because we begin, *by Sappho,* alive

Crush #90

After Childe Hassam's *Big Ben*

Something of a mystery. Heels click & echo
before step's hitch, musing. This crowd
is vine black & off to their brandies or supper,

streetlamps & carriage lights. Cadmium yellow's
allure, crushed pigment, gum Arabic from sable
or goat hair, transparent, thin & luminous.

Although you know it's clearly London—Westminster's
blue-grey wash, Parliament Houses, Big Ben,
motion's smudge, the Thames unseen, fused reflection,

lit beyond —the street's wet sheen buoyed up
in Chinese white, a blurred warmth beckons—Chicago!
Bobbie Lewis plays the Back Room & bottles

of Moet Chandon or Veuve Clicquot pass
among beautiful people who lean into necks
& dark. Ice-fogged martinis, beer caps snap, Chanel

floats in, the music starts. A name & number
inked to napkin, bled through, watery. Or
the Gold Star, Rainbo, the Matchbox where Dale

& Garin & Anto & I belly up, dry
off, tell stories, impressions of stories: the stain
& print of the rubber dress she wore that night,

stripped & eye-blacked Breedlove's *I love you, I love*
you, I love...echoing river's drift. Chocolate's
trace, Greek icons, Halsted's taverna lights, cars'

12

bass & sirens among avenues beyond
copper spires. A skyline in which we place
ourselves—London town or Chicago? Evening

caverned in reflection, rain & city's
refraction, subdue, alter, crash, or crease,
a pash, some drink, which crowd, or this—

Anne Defines *Crush* in Our 37th Year

Hook to the body,
evidence of living.
Fecund beings
without slot, niche, compartment, place,
dodging rank:
box or line or form,
a hole
(as for pigeons, notebooks, bills).
No matter
what year we are
always 14 or 22
or fill in your own crushing age—powder,
Paris, baby you
thumped against,
sucked in & white-knuckled against
that he or she might pass by everything
beginning or
nearly ending again:

A Crush after Neruda

y que subía a mi boca, /a mis manos, / una eléctrica / flor
—Pablo Neruda's "El Colegio de Invierno"

When the Southern
Cross returns or the Dipper buckles,

our mouths might crackle, our thighs
twitch & stink.

When Tecún Umán's
cigars rise zenith & plunge

to flamboyan, we'll name each gleaming
nail (the crescent

still shining mainly
for cats) & dance—black our feet with ash,

stagger in the fruit, follow maps
on your chest to a house

where a sea exhales in spring
tides. We will teem & spool

in dark. Will
the voltaic, the omnivorous.

Crush Lesson

Morris: my 10 year
old Elvis
croons & blows
necks' sweet down
under yellow pine
just outside
Miss Renfrow's sightline:
cowlick &
studied swagger, in-
tractable—
Moment's abridged
recall swivels,
twisting past:
       I've been so lonely
        I could die

A Crush for Us All Back Then

Games of small consequence in which we checked
"yes" or "no" or "maybe," as in *Will you go*

with me? Do you like me? Boxes' bright foil
& the heart's rough cut-outs; Eros, called

"Cupid" just a baby then that little rascal, chubby
as Spanky, a charming Alfalfa (Darla's valentine-

shaped face, arching & scrunching cartoonish
seduction). Something to play at, a secret

cupped at ear, chanted & rhymed, rope-skipped:
what's

                    his name?

A Crush for Jeanne

say whatever
you do behind
your velvet
Elvis is
your own biz

Crush #28

I like the look of your
big fat arms, legs like pools
for god's sake, buck & wing

with me, let me die dying
of dengue to the radio,
swear fastballs mercurial

as rainsqualls in blue over
blue, smudging these dogwoods,
sleeping wet moons,

every swallow crying
come home, come home,
save yourself for a wedding—

Wearing sling-backs
this world is tiny, impatient
these branches, this light,

balconies painted in sweet basil,
& girls, the girls buoyed,
their trembling skirts

A Crush in Dream Time

You know you should say *fruta bomba*
but whisper *papaya* because it's nasty,
repeat *Teaching! Schedule!* Where,
where's the ardor? Why this rush & rigor,
this cumulo-nimbus, this quandary
elsewhere? Shouldn't liaisons appear in rooms
with balconies & languor? Why not
Pedro with his bright teeth, open collar,
cupping history lessons to an ear— Who knows
what will expire in an hour, who knows if
there was a window or if it was flocked
in neighbors that night, gathered in blackouts,
one generator, *telenovela's*
reruns— Were sherry glasses laid out
like a sickle? An electric life-sized saint?
Was a small child in red panties outside
your door whispering *what's this what's this?*

Crush #52

[Photographs] *are the proof that something was there and no longer is. Like a stain. The stillness is boggling.*
—Diane Arbus, letter to Davis Pratt

Window. Mirror.
Wherever your own
aberrant image
catches. Wherever
all else recedes.
Cheekbone. Pallium.
A lip protrudes.
A line of vision
recognizes some
quick shape *there*.
It slips another passage
as he said you did
that raw, unfettered night.

Crush #421

It was one of those years: fallow, dry, insipid, an exsiccative
fall breeding winter, torrefying, glistening, sluggish. Afternoons

withered talk-less, nothing to story. Words crackled off stalks,
blown to corners; phrases like dust motes, ephemeral,

a feverish child. Parched, exhausted without tale or romance,
idyll, pastoral. Even the song drained, the chant emptied.

A message appeared in my inbox: *armpit & luminescent
& hoary.* That was all it took. I woke greening like Stanley Park.

Words kept coming: *pudenda, tuber, torus, cavetto,* arcing Mombasa's
rooftops; rocking & rolling, a dhow on the Indian Ocean; bursting

the cracks of Ashland Ave., taken for a Near West-Side hooker
disguised as a school girl: *gob smacked, corm, hough & helix*

& where & here & you, you, you. Then oh god & desperately
& make a clean breast of, wilting righteous, sprawling before me.

I slouched in internet cafes talking to rain, my inbox empty.
Alone, waterfalls read *Prohibir Actividades Amorosas* & college kids

from Poughkeepsie bought the beer: Pollution is a dirty means
to a radiant sunset like your smile & You must be tired—you've been

running through my mind all night & *Wanna fuck?* Crossed legs
on a bus back to the city through cloud forests; rivering, their stories

germinated, coalesced—what grows shared— bromeliads, bougainvillea,
bleeding hearts: *bract & spine, caudex & corolla, stamen,*

calyx, carpel. Sitting at a bar next to a man with hair
the color of speech & honey & semen, his appetite

straight-up Dionysian. He said: *You're hot.*

Crush #320

...high heels click into evening along sidewalk just outside this
basement window above these words assembled on a page:
Please   *please*
please   *please....*

O where are you off to
tonight?

Crush #1,011

Was it the story I told:
Her pink maillot
in his bakery
window   that listed
your ear *this* way?   Or

your guttural, some slit
fricative my chair
swiveled towards?

Saturday Night Crush, Tortugüero

Sshh against
eggs' clutch,
she spades &

flippers sand.
Then sea. Carapace,
plastron,

a pre-historic
groaning, labored
return—

Lightning
down this
natal beach,

percussion pumped
up from town,
milk-bright, Cygnus

strives south
(while "tweens"
chat *Smallville*'s

finale). What
strikes terror
as when you see

me see you
dig the scoop
of my blouse

Postcard Crushes

1.

Dear, the sun plumbs Quito & these roses.
Quiteñas in Prague's golden Christmas
beads, everywhere. I clutch at petals.

2.

Hey— I'm lost
in signs again:
Danger de Nuit!
(All moose & curve.)
If I'm lucky
Old Woman Bay
in two days—

3.

Barges trawl
this Hudson.
Scrawling you
here. Confluence
is chance is (like)
dandelions, poems.

4.

Farms of landscape
between us.
Maybe why
we both hanker
to dance
a rhythm only
insects can play?

Crush above Gold Star Boulevard

i.

Half-erased: a sweater chalked "fable,"
              your shoulder smudged in "palsied"
& December stalks
hydrangea's papery
              globes from this window
of lights & plastic.
Violet, my vision cambers.

ii.

If you ask we might say:
"Blackstrap" & don't look back—
or *Kiss me...*

but never *next Sunday*
nor *this April*

3 Crushes, Worcester

i.

Once named Hygeia Street
(Goddess of Hygiene, daughter
of Asclepius, known for his toes
& snakes & cures). Now plain
Barbara Lane beneath a blond
smoke-stack, painted brick,
halos of fog & creosote down
hill from Vincent's where he
might have kissed her in a pink
neon spell: *THIS IS IT*

ii.

Franklin Street's train cars & tracks
abandoned. Cantaloupe rinds off
Arctic Street, boxed, read: *Canuck*
Rutabagas Washed & Waxed.
A wooden hand poised
within chain links, proffers air
above Our Lady; a tribute to fire
& loss. Plastic poinsettias wreathe
a single wine glass & above all:
                    Keep Out Keep Out

iii.

Yet, night
in its turnings,
a face half-
deflects the lights
in mine, shifts all:
paper birch & moonseed
edge some old mill pond
or *There*—
  where my buddy
got the shit beat outta him—

A Crush for Paris & Oenone

After the painting by Pieter Lastman

Country faces. She's between sit and lean,
into or against him, yielding her body's weight
& breadth—no small thing for a woman these days.
His left hand half cups half clutches her breast,
a pleasure to himself....

        Not sure I would like
being half-naked & felt up in a pasture
in view of the faithful dog & farm couple,
but his thigh & bicep are Brando as Kowalski
& I am amazed how much I
love men, careless to the bad
times that shine around the bend:
                goats & bagpipes,
dark vines lolling darkness,
                         that other woman

Crush #19

the cinema is cruel / like a miracle
            —Frank O'Hara's "An Image of Leda"

Her smirk & catch poised before a cigarette,
his con's eye & lips working toothpick,
the locked door, the absent husband,
loaves & dough still perfect or rising,
his face implied in her thighs' diamond,
palm's thrust, knife flung, *C'mon*—
helping him help himself to shank
of neck, kneading breasts, the garter,
her stockings, his grip & squeeze between,
a tight shot the camera won't release
until we, we— wonder: is this love
for Cora Papadakis & Frank
Chambers where the heart is crushed
vagabond & bound, resuscitated
in lust, when at a roadside station,
they wait for neon, drink coffee,
how she says *do I look Greek to you?*

A Crush on the Venus of Willendorf

A contradiction, as beauty
is or can be. Delicate,
adipose, unruly,
coy—belly, breasts, thighs
pressed
       encased,
we crescent her. Knees fricase, feet
shift, shuffle, impossible
to pull out, away from this
story before story: *Magna mater?*
Divine whore?

Crush #49

A space must be maintained or desire ends.
—Anne Carson

about your knees he whispered

above the hough, above the tongue

across certain palms

after evaporation, lacy & leaf-like

against oil derricks, the dark undazzle

along the avenue, hair toss & fuck all

among a scumbling of colors

around, glittering with joy

at the table : *you're beautiful   you're beautiful   pass me the pepper*

before I go

behind the dunes

below the belt

beneath alabaster, vitrified

beside himself

between sacrum & ilium

by gum

down river

during gibbous moons

except Vienna & Paris

for this poem

from the 12 strings to my heart

in rough sheets three times or more

in auricles, in airports

inside the stall beneath

instead of a kiss

into the south of it

like her petunias

near(er) she said

of moustache to helix

off the charts

on the lawn, paler than condoms' gleam

on top of her nightstand

onto the next thing

out of chants & variation

outside windows, that entering takes away

over & over & over (again)

past Arcturus

since April is

through corners we dance

to Halsted & Taylor

towards geometry

under enormous pressure of circumstance

underneath, yes, underneath

until Cooley came to town

up Lisa Lane

upon learning "My Foolish Heart"

with him not there—

within ear's hive

without him—   she hears him, she sees

Bridge Jumping/ W4M / Poughkeepsie
(The Walkway)

You smelled of burning maps, smirked as to *let slip the dogs of war*. Not the stale slate windbreaker & steel-cut oats above the Hudson. I was whistling "Wake Up, Little Susie" & wearing a *huipil*. Your crow's feet, tasseographical signs for *journey of hindrance, diploma*. The conversation went like giraffes fighting: *How do you behead a poem like a horse? Why is the "ch" silent in "chthonic"?* I refused your urge to push the mental health button, see what might appear: pair of falcons, oil cymes between trains, a child in a tiara. I told you the death rate was 1180 for every 1200 jumps, including Kid Courage. I told you in Hong Kong it's the most popular form. You said falling from this height blows your clothes off, denies the senses. You wondered what happened to the 20 who got away? Cross-winds, a unicycle & my Mets cap divided factors. But I keep thinking of you like Colomb & Williams thought of Wayne C. Booth, writing his voice into the third edition of *The Craft of Research* years after he died. I imagine you might fish endangered sturgeon & dream of *Guernica* on Thursdays. If so, write to me. We could go to sea in a sieve, double the blind, buck your tiger, bell my cat, leap this dark—

Kalends/December

Horseshoe crab & yellow
pine, quick gifts locked in a trunk.

The Atlantic so cold
it numbs my fantasy

of stripping here & now
to relive his youth. Gulls wheel

& *gowl*. Gannets plunge-
dive beyond sightlines.

Detritus arcs & fish
crows in the dunes.

When I say *kiss me*
I leave my glasses on

Crush from Ottawa

A new city in a new
   year after hotel sex
   & oranges (as

abracadabra on
parchment for tooth-aches.)
    I say "*oscillate* from

tiny masks blown among
grapevines." He says "it's moonshine
    spells nonsense." Once called "Bytown,"

"adawe" & "grand or
decorated ears," *Vincent ate*
   Tammy in black, that wall over there

Nones/January

Wine has no rudder & so we drink
vodka tonics, watch motions of this bay:

Current's brow, contracts moustache
to collar, radial. A face buried just

above the occipital bone, breathes
salt, summer hay, a small nest & respite

from cold in the 18th hour. We
fidget rough sheets, a dry heat. I story

sex with other men to stop from—

Winter's Crush

Before us this fabled moon sprouting
kale. The *seet & caw* notch at window, flare
yard's cherry, pear. We *wait*. In your childhood

language it is the same word as *hope*.
We sleep in swells & testa burst, lengthen
downward before bed's tug & world. The dog star,

trips across sky
                    & a vinyl
seat where I wait for you to cleave, pull me in-
to—

Crushed in February

Month of the dead.
Month of wool & wolves & wolf whistles.
Month whipped through the streets.
O pine branch, O grain roasted with salt.
Anything can be purified.

A Crush before the Sexual Revolution

Now that I'm old this cold freezes the quarter notes of my thought.
Memory's just a jacklight of *once*. I used to hide wings & eggs, damaged
things, in a crawl space beneath the house. Colors lived in my eyes

as rejection. I stowed a pocket watch & buckeyes beneath
a sycamore, the clouds of Worcester. My favorite word:
mercurial. I've been summoned through Pig Alley, scanned lavender

fields on the Isle of Wight. I spied a neighbor girl peeing
a ditch when I was ten. Her skirt's hitch & crooked mouth survive.
It's like a hummingbird's quicksilver jab to a red vest.

These are bones in my soup, nevertheless. My father danced
a gimpy box step. My mother stole apples from Kunitz's
tree. One May, I photographed Priscilla in gingham & pearls.

She sang "sugar, cause sugar never was so sweet." At the edge
of Bell Pond. At the edge of Bell Pond. Later that summer she
beaded her thighs with my initials. *She carved them there.*

One for April

It's not easy coming back from the dead
each year to lilac's febrile pull, a wild

push of styptic plum & dogwood's blood-plashed
petals—a press to mull: *blemish, ration;*

the language shoves, our shoulders put to: *door,*
cellar door, cellar door—can you hear it?

The most beautiful sounds mysterious
fidelity to our ears, we linger:

in linguals, to dentals, what gutturals
tunnel this radix of time & place: that radish

or wool, turniped but heaving the blue, roots
the way it goes

Crushed in Poughkeepsie Time

What is seen here/folding over itself/is a gathering of those /
pasts we voyage into
        —Michael Anania's "River Songs of Arion I-X"

Whale-rending along these shores leads us to South Seas, a silk factory,
hotel burnings; like dreams' net or currents one with another—

hemlock-black, brackish & lovely, fresh or tang, estuary's switch.
That all time cannot exist at once in our heads: cigar-making & electric

trolleys, how you bent & sighed into your shoes, peeled oranges
in a shape of eyes. What is forgotten lingers, the "lion-headed store front,"

bobs or busts through this now, a warning without warning,
can you dig it, a buoy of the past, place-marker & maker, tricked out

as "picking your feet" in *The French Connection*, cough drops called "Trade"
& "Mark," rising high school rafters in Marian Anderson's contralto.

Imagine histories current: ferries trawl nigh 300 years; Brando haunts
Happy Jack's on Northbridge Street. We might say Poughkeepsie

& hear "reed-covered lodge near the place of the little-water,"
"the Queen City," "safe & pleasant harbor," *look & see* the Pequod chief

& his beloved spooning in the shade. This river sailing the Half-Moon
back to Crusades, a city spelled 42 ways & young Vassar brewing

in Newburgh. Rio San Gomez is the Mauritius is the Muheakantuck is
the Lordly Hudson, place of the deepest water & river

of the steep hills—what if we are still dancing in Chicago's hottest summer
as Wappingi braves are coming up the path & Van Kleek's house

just yonder Fall Kill? You are writing me letters from Rio Dulce & I
am eating bagels at the Reo Diner. Modjeski sits imagining this bridge;

his mother swoons as Juliet in Crakow. At night the lights of these still
busy foundries become strange fires, beckoning America—&

maybe not; their great furnaces' ambient noise, soughing across these waters;
concurrent worlds asleep, dreaming, not dreaming

Archaic Crush

Let it take you
   where it leads—
     Aphrodite,

herself, in arms
   of gorgeous War;
     Hephaestus,

the shuffling husband,
   watching at bedside,
     & magically

by magic loosened,
   before awkward
     exits, to bathe, recover....

The Jews, the Christians,
   wanted meaning
     in every *thing* or act,

to see God, perhaps,
   to know biblically.
     Troubling, isn't it?

(Crushed in) the *Sea of Love*

or was it
Happiness
where we dipped,
a park away
from a library
that night
the sea of
the wonder
still in my ear
as bright plastic fish
swimming oak
laminate
as our heads
in round after
round— *Poets*
we all said
& I wanted
to tell you
then   *O*
just how much

Crush 9W: A Fable

Once there was a silver hearse with a black
steer mounted on top that her ex-mother-in-law
drove, delivering Frank's Steakhouse
along 9W's décolletage & ditching family
pets to mountainsides, gullies:
two gerbils, four cats, a pot-bellied pig.
To that end, her ex stole himself to Syracuse,
Buffalo, Boston, further each time,
abandoned sidewalk railings, assorted
shelving, low ceilings & tenants,
their chickens, rheumatic children,
the gasping bedbugs of Brooklyn.

Crush, Texas

Planned demolition
never goes the way
we think it will.

Arrogance before
locomotion
& some dude proclaiming

himself "Agent Crush"
on a prancing charger,
two dollars a head,

the bearded princess,
Medicine shows, a sword-
swallowing baby.

The Coming Attraction:
carnage, wreckage—
a photographer's

eye lost & the rest,
smoking souvenirs.
What kids these days

call a *hot mess.*

Crush on a Road Trip

The myth in America—things move:
Poverty lines & flamingos blush
to blackjacks & sumac, dashboard

hula girls mug at spinners, these night-
crawlers & minnows. *Mike + Lisa*
4Ever red on a water tower

adorn Friendship, Winslow, Welch or Asheville;
loblollies & felt-covered dogs bob *right*
on; peanut brittle & roadside zoos,

chicory & horseshoes voo-doo these chiggers.
There's sorghum for sale. Mad Dog & cullet
grade this road; pet rocks & mood rings mushroom

in Grape Crush, Red Man & Wing Dings—
whatever you might wish along
the Mississippi. Mules drown &

flogging spots spell romance in the voice
of Mr. Moon River *wherever you're going*
we're going your way. Go Fish across

vinyl seats. *Someone's in the kitchen with*
Dinah. Jimmy crack corn & I spy chrome
of a Nomad—   or was that a Rambler?

Crush for a Once Sestina

O these sestinas jest / they cleave the hopsack
with know-how to browbeat
the latchkey / the tell-alls

Crochet the septums / & pub-crawl
scrawl the ample, outspread broad
crusade these wattles

Persuade rucksacks / squeegee the scatback
They nickname dead seas, nutgalls / A-frame us
in cul-de-sacs (our nodding gimcracks)
free-fall Rockaway / flank the zodiac, Mumbai

But for seawalls / & razorbacks
they could parboil chick-peas / go tenure-track
draft umiaks / counter-claim catcalls

O lawdy Miss Maudy! / is this the Tao
of Arnault Daniel? / or envois
up in the Armagnac?

Shellac the plimsolls! / confit the nightshade!
These sestinas / swaybacked
Neanderthals & coryphées
stink of menthol, meatballs / they deliquesce
they merengue

We will stop
& smell / the sumac
yoke with them

Crush #40

Someday we will become Mrs. Robinson.
We will slip a clip-on off an earlobe to take a call.

Our penciled eyebrows will insist it is 1967.
This is the year of our births which we carefully

fail to mention across the bar from him or her,
scruffy & smooth, young like we remember

believing we would always be.
Not just young looking. Like Elaine

& Benjamin we shall take a bus bound
for someplace other than this age.

Crushed Psalms

Let us gown the red shower curtain
Let us eight track the gospel
Let us double modal & apocopate
Let us tump & perfoliate
Let us call the hogs to scattered examples of fair dialect
As cowbrute so whickerbill
As winter water so skillet tea
Let us climb the tower for a dime & pie
Let us fry the grindle, pickle the gar
Let bone from water & roads of cullet
Let three deep & no lack of corky protrusion
Let K-Tel present the Everly Brothers
Let us "Dream, Dream, Dream"
Let Pistol Gunn come to town,
his Dentyne & gold incisor, his white patent leather.
Let not the girdle nor the mouth of soap
Let us praise Tang & curlers at noon
Let us gin our Dixies
Let us cuss from innocence
As we hymn so shall we holler
As we panicle so shall we spike
Let us impeach our mouths
Let the long "S" of her hair
Let stickers bush & ass pie
May she pull up in her mama's Impala, smoking Camels
May we be thirteen, an empty house
Let us eulogize the candy bars of Piggly Wiggly
Let us sit under the toothache tree with the prom king of poetry
Let "Arkansas Snap"
Let *that* dog hunt
Let us decoupage Jesus at the door
Let us to the five points of Calvinism
Let not the heat, but humidity's sweet flank

Let Frank Stanford's eyes "shine for twenty dollar shoes... like
possum brains on the good road"
Let finger bones of Pea Ridge trumpet honeysuckle
Let the Hard-shelled Baptists we've loved before
Let us belly bob wire, escape by hoopsnake
May there be a bed of devil's food & 7UP cake
May we kick the can of death
May we walk perimeters of a dare
May this geography guard our going out & our coming in
May all our days reckon & give ear
May the dogwood in April forever, amen

Birthday Crush

Always the moon & evil spirit routine, a tick & hover.

The quick we hoard like gold anklets, plastic lids.

These are small rituals of maintenance: spank & sing & blow.

It was said: to soften the body for the grave.

Each decade "all" shimmers before us.

Wish: a shaved head, fire, the years' deep clean.

[Crushed] to Pieces

building is a product of demolition
to unhinge is also a way to open
the door
        —Catherine Kasper's "Blueprints of the City"

1.

        Creosote's

rhombus to pavement   clutch & dapple

:   lilacs' heart,   spade,

honeysuckle's   sprawling cursive,

palms

& knees   grass-stained,
                when hiding,   named

2.

Language turns
to the ocean
forgetting its
average:
64.1
pounds per
cubic foot—
enough to
crush us in
lack

3.

I know it hurts to burn
     —Adrienne Rich

In the crush-pen that year,
we learned vitality in branding:
Never mind its smell or bawl—
burning spancels us to place.

4.

I sing the body electric
     —Walt Whitman

Only three pounds of blood,
dream & electricity. To say:
I have a crush on you
slights the surging within:
a million tiny lightning storms

5.

What turns back
in
on one
word's ord,
small
destruction,
starts again: expels
shape's change

6.

Rummages & keepsakes. Maybe. Crushed
velvet, jump-suits & fishnets, odd lace or stilettos.
Made in Macau   Made in Mexico—
Sparkles, catches, dissembled, disguise.
Whatever suits her fancy.
                    Or fit.

7.

Would we
if we could
measure
pain's ratio
to a moment's
notice?

8.

Beyond Nairobi & the Rift
Valley below, hills frame this
periphery as if some god's
prudent sundering.
(See: compression, thrust, shattering)
Kristina & me, winking photographs,
Safari Njema!   :
Shifting platelets are no joke.

9.

Bywater's Disease: A crush that lingers

Crush of Poppies

Tell me the dream where we gather walnuts at heat lines,
                    dizzy flies in loose fists, croon sundown to cattle.
Our photographs: Kodak-vague & floating beds of meringue,
gingham fanning shale, a crow who might've talked, knuckle bones in the well...
          It's not like a road that leads to the wizard's house.
          It's more like hiding in our mother's closet waiting out twisters, patent
          leather purses we snapped open, shut, open,
                         breathed White Linen, wishing a loose cup
of grasses, *queedle turee*, un-sayable dehiscence.

See the dross, the dusty striated arcs. This means landing in Technicolor,
this means we gave up our pumps to the witch.
          Tell me she is us: tined & apple green,
                                   delicious

Palinode

There's no place where the dancing's free. No kissing against chicken cages.

No bloody palms & waffles. Nor the stain of a rubber dress.

No eye-blacked Breedlove yelling *love* down river.

Anne never defined anything at thirty-seven.

There was no story of a pink maillot in his bakery window.

No one wrote *hough or helix, torus & cavetto.* No one

mistook anyone for a Near West-Side hooker. You're silly

if you think Cooley came to town. (He's playing the fields up Winnipeg.)

Nope, no one across a table: *You're beautiful*

you're beautiful   pass me the pepper.

Cora Papadakis did say, "Do I look Greek to you?" That was the movies.

No burning maps; no one conversed like giraffes fighting.

It wasn't a trompe l'oeil, nor Vienna's glittering stilts with Stella.

That poem never got written. There was a sea turtle & percussion

& thirteen year olds discussing prime time. (But c'mon, this is poetry

& the *post*-modern world.) There were no deserted gerbils & pot-bellied

pigs on 9W. No knuckle bones in the well.

Crush, Texas was a temporary town.

I wish I'd eulogized the candy bars of Piggly Wiggly, played "Arkansas Snap."

I swear I wished for a red shower curtain gown & shifting platelets.

What have you done with my skillet tea & scattered examples of fair dialect?

Where is the prom king of poetry when you want him?

My life-sized electric saint?

How do you spot a toothache tree or kick the can of death?

Why spank & sing & blow to soften a body for the grave?

When she shows up smoking Camels in her mama's Impala, give me a call.

Should we slight the surging within? Could we

land in Technicolor or a year's deep clean?

There's story & there's story. Song sings its own answer:

Shimmy shimmy coco bop shimmy shimmy pop

Crush Starting with a Line by Jack Gilbert

Desire perishes because it tries to be love
& so, I think, why search or seek it? Entering
its way out the backdoor, calling as Narcissus
himself, curious to himself only—only

this echo. Yet, some days wild turkeys wing clumsy
across windshields, or poets come to town
& language flocks before flying south, before
jubilee, before hush & slack. In chance,

what we flush from beech & oak, or her flush blooming
at a table, remains, persists as flight, or flown:
trace of bird in my eye, balloon drift among sky,
proposing hand, arm. What is not sexual, though

sex is part, catches life *en theos.* Not love, but its
roaming kin & nonetheless, wonderful alone.

Acknowledgments

In gratitude to the editors of the following publications in which these poems first appeared, some in alternate versions & different titles:

American Letters & Commentary, American Poetry Journal, Bedside Guide to No Tell Motel, The Bedside Guide to No Tell Motel - Second Floor, Blank Canvas, Connotations Press, Fifth Wednesday, Gathering: Fifteen Poets/Poems, Moria, Mudlark, Ships That Pass Blog, The City Visible: Anthology of Chicago Poetry, The Notre Dame Review, The Peter F. Yacht Club #11 and *The Worcester Review*.

Also, some of these poems appear in *Calendar Girls*, a chapbook published by above/ground press in 2006.

I am deeply grateful to Reb Livingston for her spunk & savvy & support. Also, I owe a great poetic debt to Jill Alexander Essbaum for her astute editorial skills and generosity. Thank you both for helping *dar la luz* to this work. Many thanks to Mary Behm-Steinberg, who channeled the spirit of this book.

I am thankful to Michael Anania for his experience, wisdom & friendship & even more for his patience & generosity to me through the years.

A special thanks to my friend & colleague, Tommy Zurhellen, who consistently read & encouraged this book. (I'm holdin' on, TZ, I'm holdin' on!)

Thanks to Adam Williams for his critical eye and astute reading of this book near the end (& for Ella & Billie, who helped somehow).

Thanks to my family & my creative community: Brian Clements, Dennis Cooley, Garin & Shadla Cycholl, Gino DiIorio, Stephen

DiRado, Kristina Dziedzic Wright, Anne Geller, rob mclennan &
John Q. Monteramour.

"Postcard Crushes" is dedicated to rob mclennan.
"Crush #421" is in gratitude to Jason Emde.
"3 Crushes, Worcester" is in memoriam to the six firefighters who
lost their lives in the warehouse fire, 1999.
"Crush 9W: A Fable" is dedicated to Elizabeth Weaver.
"Crush, Texas" is in gratitude to Gabby Albino.
"Crush for a Once Sestina" is after Fenn Stewart.
"Crushed in Poughkeepsie Time" is dedicated to Javier Crespo.
"Crushed Psalms" is dedicated to Bill Allegrezza & Ray Bianci.
"Crush of Poppies" is dedicated to Joanne Anania.
"Palinode" is in gratitude to Brian Clements.

"Crushed: A Preface": All definitions of "crush" come from the
Oxford English Dictionary.
"Where the dancing's free" is the rewritten version of Tom Waits'
"Jersey Girl" by Bruce Springsteen.
"Within the precincts of the poem" is from Reginald Shepherd's
final blog posting.
"Stirring beyond your wall" is from Michael Anania's *Continuous
Showings*.
"I'm not a player I just crush a lot" is from Big Punisher's *Still Not
a Player*: (radio edit), songwriters: Carlos Manuel Rios & Jerome
Foster.
"No sight & drumming" is from Sappho's "Fragment 31" & "in the
absences of eyes" is from Aeschylus's *Agamemnon*. Both are quoted
in Anne Carson's *Eros: The Bittersweet*.

"Crush on a Road Trip": "the myth in America is that things move"
is from Garin Cycholl's *Rafetown Georgics*, page 19.

"Crushed Psalms" : "shining for twenty dollar shoes..." is from Frank
Stanford's *The Battlefield Where the Moon Says I Love You*, page 9.

"Crush Starting with a Line by Jack Gilbert" is from Jack Gilbert's
The Great Fires.

About the Author

Photo Credit: Jay Graham

Lea Graham is a native of Northwest Arkansas. She is the author of the chapbook, *Calendar Girls* (above/ground press, 2006). Her poems, collaborations, reviews and articles have been published in journals and anthologies such as *American Letters & Commentary, The Bedside Guide to No Tell Motel - Second Floor, Notre Dame Review* and *The Capilano Review.* Her translations are forthcoming in *The Alteration of Silence: Recent Chilean Poetry* through the University of New Orleans Press. She is Assistant Professor of English at Marist College in Poughkeepsie, New York.

Also by No Tell Books

2010
Glass Is Really a Liquid, by Bruce Covey
God Damsel, by Reb Livingston

2009
PERSONATIONSKIN, by Karl Parker

2008
Cadaver Dogs, by Rebecca Loudon

2007
The Bedside Guide to No Tell Motel - Second Floor,
        editors Reb Livingston & Molly Arden
Harlot, by Jill Alexander Essbaum
Never Cry Woof, by Shafer Hall
Shy Green Fields, by Hugh Behm-Steinberg
The Myth of the Simple Machines, by Laurel Snyder

2006
The Bedside Guide to No Tell Motel, editors Reb Livingston
      & Molly Arden
Elapsing Speedway Organism, by Bruce Covey
The Attention Lesson, by PF Potvin
Navigate, Amelia Earhart's Letters Home, by Rebecca Loudon
Wanton Textiles, by Reb Livingston & Ravi Shankar

notellbooks.org